£1

The Ultimate
M U F F I N
R E C I P E   B O O K

Delightful Muffin Recipes For Beginners

By
Les Ilagan

Table of Contents

INTRODUCTION 6

Homemade Banana Muffins 9

Pineapple Carrot Muffins With Walnuts........11

Banana Cashew Muffins................................13

Yummy Banana Cinnamon Muffins 15

Cheesy Lemon Muffins..................................17

Crumbled Cherry Rhubarb Muffin With
Walnuts 19

Chocolate Muffin Overload 22

Rich Chocolate Muffin...................................24

Chocolate Almond Muffin 26

Triple Chocolate Muffins................................28

Easy Vanilla Buttermilk Muffins 30

Homemade Orange Muffins with Cinnamon .32

Chocolate Chip Muffins.................................34

Blueberry Almond Muffins............................36

Carrot and Raisin Muffins 38

Pumpkin Spice Banana Muffins....................41

Buttered Corn Muffins 43

Homemade Almond Muffins 45

Banana Cashew Muffins...............................47

Yummy Peppermint Chocolate Muffins.........49

Cherry Almond Meal Muffin 51

Fluffy Chocolate Muffins 53

Choco Walnut Muffins 56

Blueberry and Vanilla Muffin 58

Banana Oat and Raisin Muffins 60

Coconut and Lemon Muffins 63

Poppy Seed Muffins with Applesauce 65

Pumpkin and Pecan Muffins 67

Banana Walnut Muffins 70

Delicious Ban apple Muffins with Almonds ...73

Homemade Blackberry and Oat Muffins 76

Vanilla Almond Muffin 78

Easy Banana Oat Muffin................................80

Coffee Choco Muffins....................................82

Luscious Cranberry Muffin with Flaxseed 84

Easy Nutella Muffins 86

Orange Blueberry Muffins with Hemp Seeds .89

Homemade Muffins with Sour Cream 91

Banana Peanut Butter Muffins......................93

Sweet Chocolate Muffins with Honey 95

Buttermilk Muffins with Chocolate Chips 97

Deep Dark Chocolate Muffins 99

Cheesy Muffins 101

Choco Coffee Muffins with Cinnamon 103

Super Moist Banana and Pumpkin Muffins..105

Cheese Muffins with Vanilla........................**107**

Cranberry Pineapple Muffins with Walnuts.**109**

Homemade Bran Muffins with Flaxseeds **111**

Orange Ginger Muffins................................**113**

Yummy Party Chocolate Muffins **115**

INTRODUCTION

This book offers easy muffin recipes that even beginners can make. You'll find here delectable muffin recipes from blueberry to corn to chocolate chip and everything in between!

This book has many wonderful muffin recipes that you will surely enjoy baking as well as eating with your loved ones.

Muffins are somewhat similar to cupcakes in terms of size, texture and taste. But you must know that muffins are not mini cakes, they are more like mini quick breads because they are denser and less sweet as compared to cupcakes. In most cases, muffins do not come with icing or frosting on top, instead they are plain or with crumbled topping. Also, if the recipe requires - the fruits, nuts, or chocolate chips are already incorporated in the batter to be enjoyed later on as you take each bite.

Never miss out on the all-time favorite Banana Walnut Muffins, Deep Dark Chocolate Muffins, Pumpkin Spice Banana Muffins, Blueberry Almond Muffins, and other delightful flavors.

Muffins can either be sweet or savory. These little quick breads are fun to make because you can add up different kind of ingredients to enhance the flavor of your muffins. They are perfect to have for breakfast, snack, lunch, picnic item, or to serve at parties. You can also put them in a box and send as presents to your family and friends.

This book is a part of many cookbook series that I am writing; I hope you have fun trying all the recipes in this book. So now, let's get started!

Homemade Banana Muffins

Simple yet tasty muffin recipe with remarkable banana flavor that everyone will surely enjoy.

Preparation Time: 10 minutes
Total Time: 40 minutes
Yield: 18servings

Ingredients

3 ripe bananas (mashed)
1/4cup brown sugar
1large egg (lightly beaten)
1/3cup canola oil
1 cup milk
2cups whole wheat flour

2 teaspoons baking powder
1 teaspoon baking soda
¼ teaspoon salt

Method

1.   Preheat your oven to 350F. Line muffin trays with paper cups.

2.   In a large bowl, mix together the bananas and brown sugar until smooth using an electric mixer. Add the egg, milk and oil; beat until blended.

3.   Add the whole wheat flour, baking powder, baking soda, and salt. Mix until just combined.

4.   Pour batter into the muffin cups, about 3/4 full.

5.   Bake in the oven for 20-25 minutes or until tested done. Place in wire racks to cool.

6.   Serve or store in airtight container.

Pineapple Carrot Muffins With Walnuts

This muffin recipe has a healthy combination of pineapple, carrots, and walnuts.

Preparation Time: 15minutes
Total Time: 40 minutes
Yield: 24servings

Ingredients

1 medium egg (lightly beaten)
1/3 cup canola oil
1/3 cup granulated sugar
3/4 cup milk
3/4 cup carrots (grated)

1/4 cup crushed pineapple
1 teaspoon vanilla extract
1 1/2 cups all-purpose flour
1/2 cup rolled oats
2 1/2 teaspoons baking powder
1 teaspoon baking soda
1/2 teaspoon salt
1/2 cup walnuts (chopped)

Method

1.   Preheat your oven to 350 F. Line muffin trays with paper cups.

2.   In a large bowl, mix together the egg, canola oil, sugar, milk, carrot, pineapple, and vanilla extract until well blended.

3.   Add the flour, rolled oats, baking powder, baking soda, and salt. Mix until just combined. Fold in walnuts.

4.   Pour batter into the muffin cups, about 3/4 full.

5.   Bake in the oven for 20-25 minutes or until tested done. Place in wire racks to cool.

6.   Serve or store in airtight container.

Banana Cashew Muffins

A tasty and easy to make muffin recipe with bananas and cashews.

Preparation Time: 15minutes
Total Time: 40 minutes
Yield: 22servings

Ingredients

1/4 cup brown sugar
1/4 cup butter (unsalted)
1large egg (beaten)
3 medium ripe bananas (mashed)
1 cup buttermilk
1 teaspoon vanilla extract
2 cups whole wheat flour (sifted)

½ teaspoon salt
1 teaspoon baking powder
1 teaspoon baking soda
1 cup dry roasted cashew nuts

Method

1. Preheat the oven to 350F. Line muffin trays with paper cups.

2. In a bowl, cream together sugar and butter. Add the egg, bananas, buttermilk, and vanilla extract. Mix well.

3. Sift the whole wheat flour, baking powder, baking soda, and salt; add into the wet mixture. Mix until just combined. Fold in half of the cashews.

4. Pour batter into the muffin cups, about 3/4full. Sprinkle with remaining cashews.

5. Bake in the oven for 20-25 minutes or until tested done. Place in wire racks to cool.

6. Serve and enjoy.

Yummy Banana Cinnamon Muffins

A delightful banana muffin recipe with cinnamon.

Preparation Time: 15minutes
Total Time: 40 minutes
Yield: 20servings

Ingredients

1/4 cup brown sugar
1/4 cup vegetable oil
1large egg
3mashed ripe banana

1/2 cup sour cream
1/2 cup milk
2 cups whole wheat flour
2 ½ teaspoons baking powder
1 teaspoon baking soda
½ teaspoon salt
1 teaspoon ground cinnamon
Powdered sugar (for dusting)

Method

1.   Preheat your oven to 350F. Line muffin trays with paper cups.

2.   Using a wire whisk, mix together the brown sugar, oil and egg in a large bowl. Add the mashed bananas, sour cream, and milk. Mix well.

3.   Stir in the dry ingredients until just blended. Pour batter in muffin cups evenly, about 3/4full.

7.   Bake in the oven for 20-25 minutes or until tested done. Place in wire racks to cool.

8.   Dust muffins with powdered sugar.

4.   Serve and enjoy.

Cheesy Lemon Muffins

A great tasting muffin recipe with cheese and a hint of lemon.

Preparation Time: 15minutes
Total Time: 40 minutes
Yield: 24servings

Ingredients

2 cups all-purpose flour, sifted
2 teaspoon baking powder
1 teaspoon baking soda
1/3 cup unsalted butter
1 large egg
1 cup milk
1/2 cup cream cheese

1/2 cup condensed milk
1/4 cup fresh lemon juice
1 teaspoon lemon zest
1/2 cup cheddar cheese (grated)

Method

1.   Preheat your oven to 350F. Line muffin trays with paper cups.

2.   Mix together the all-purpose flour, baking powder, and baking soda in a medium bowl.

3.   In a separate bowl, beat cream cheese until fluffy. Add the butter, egg, condensed milk, lemon juice, and zest.

4.   Gradually add the flour mixture; mix until just combined.

5.   Fold in cheddar cheese until incorporated.

6.   Pour batter in muffin cups, about 3/4full.

7.   Bake in the oven for about 20-25minutes or until tested done. Cool in wire racks.

8.   Serve and enjoy.

Crumbled Cherry Rhubarb Muffin With Walnuts

This muffin recipe combines the amazing flavors of rhubarb, cherries, and almonds.

Preparation Time: 15 minutes
Total Time: 40 minutes
Yield: 20servings

Ingredients

2cups all-purpose flour
2 ½ teaspoon baking powder
1 teaspoon baking soda

1/4 cup sugar
1/4 teaspoon salt
1large egg (lightly beaten)
1 cup milk
½ cup vegetable oil
½ cup rhubarb (coarsely chopped)
½ cup cherry (pitted and chopped)

For Crumble Topping:
1/3 cup almonds (coarsely chopped)
1/3 cup whole wheat flour
1/3 cup packed brown sugar
1/4 teaspoon cinnamon
3 tablespoons butter

Method

1.   Preheat your oven to 350F. Line the muffin trays with paper cups.

2.   In a large bowl, mix together the flour, baking powder, baking soda, sugar, and salt.

3.   In a separate bowl, combine milk, egg, and oil. Pour into flour mixture and mix with a wire whisk until moistened and smooth. Fold in rhubarb and cherries.

4.   Pour batter to muffin cups, about3/4full.

5.   Combine   crumble   topping ingredients in a small bowl.

6.   Top each muffin cup with crumble topping.

7.   Bake in the oven for 20 to 25 minutes or until golden and tested done. Cool in wire racks.

8.   Serve and enjoy.

Chocolate Muffin Overload

These chocolate muffins make great snack for the kids, they will love it!

Preparation Time: 15 minutes
Total Time: 45 minutes
Yield: 20 servings

Ingredients

2 cups all-purpose flour
2 teaspoons baking powder
1teaspoon baking soda
1/2 cup cocoa powder
1/2cup brown sugar
1/2cup buttermilk
1/2 cup hot water
1/2cup butter (melted)

1 large egg
1 teaspoon vanilla extract
1 cup semisweet chocolate chips
(divided)

Method

1.   Preheat in the oven to 350F. Line the muffin trays with baking cups.

2.   In a large mixing bowl, combine the flour, baking powder, baking soda, cocoa powder, and brown sugar.

3.   Combine all the wet ingredients in a separate bowl.

4.   Mix together the dry and wet ingredients until just combined.

5.   Fold in half of the chocolate chips.

6.   Pour batter to muffin cups, about 3/4 full. Top with remaining chocolate chips.

7.   Bake in the oven for 20-25 minutes or until tested done. Cool in wire racks.

8.   Serve or store in airtight container.

Rich Chocolate Muffin

This is a delicious and very easy chocolate muffin recipe that even your kids will enjoy doing.

Preparation Time: 15minutes
Total Time: 40 minutes
Yield: 18servings

Ingredients
2cups whole wheat flour
2 teaspoons baking powder
1 teaspoon baking soda
1/2 cup cocoa powder
1/2 cup brown sugar
1/2 teaspoon salt

1 cup water
1/2 cup vegetable oil
1 teaspoon white vinegar
Chocolate shavings (for topping)

Method

1.   Preheat the oven to 350F. Line the muffin trays with baking cups.

2.   In a large bowl, combine the whole wheat flour, baking powder, baking soda, cocoa powder, sugar and salt.

3.   Whisk together the water, oil, and vinegar in a separate bowl.

4.   Combine the dry and wet ingredients until just blended and lump-free.

5.   Pour batter into muffin cups, about 3/4full. Sprinkle with chocolate shavings.

6.   Bake in the oven for 20-25 minutes or until tested done. Place in wire racks to cool.

7.   Serve or store in airtight container.

Chocolate Almond Muffin

This muffin recipe a great combination of flavors from the chocolate and almonds. It is perfect to serve at kiddie parties.

Preparation Time: 15minutes
Total Time: 50 hour
Yield: 20servings

Ingredients

2 cups of whole wheat flour
2/3 cup of cocoa powder, unsweetened
1 ½ teaspoon of baking powder
1 teaspoon of baking soda
1/2 teaspoon of salt
1/2 cup of unsalted butter, softened
1/2 cup of brown sugar
1 large egg

1 teaspoon vanilla extract
1/2 cup water
1/2 cup almond milk
1/2 cup slivered almonds

Method

1.   Preheat the oven to 350 F. Line muffin trays with paper cups.

2.   In a large bowl, combine whole wheat flour, cocoa powder, baking powder, baking soda, and salt.

3.   Beat butter with sugar using an electric mixer until smooth and fluffy. Scrape sides of bowl.

4.   Add the egg, vanilla extract, water, and almond milk.

5.   At low speed, gradually add the flour mixture mix until just combined.

6.   Spoon batter into the muffin cups, about3/4 full. Sprinkle with slivered almonds.

7.   Bake in the oven for 20-25 minutes or when until tested done. Place in wire racks to cool.

8.   Serve and enjoy.

Triple Chocolate Muffins

Wonderful chocolate muffins topped with chocolate frosting and mini chocolate chips.

Preparation Time: 15 minutes
Total Time: 40 minutes
Yield: 20servings

Ingredients

2cups whole wheat flour
1/3 cup brown sugar
2 teaspoons baking powder
1 teaspoon baking soda
1/2 cup cocoa powder
1/2 teaspoon salt

1 cup hot water
1/2 cup vegetable oil
1 teaspoon white vinegar
Chocolate frosting (to serve)
Mini chocolate chips (white and semi-sweet)

Method

1.   Preheat your oven to 350F. Line muffin trays with baking cups.

2.   In a large bowl, combine whole wheat flour, sugar, baking soda, baking powder, cocoa powder, and salt.

3.   Add the hot water, vegetable oil, and vinegar. Mix until just blended.

4.   Pour batter to muffin cups, about 3/4 cup full only.

5.   Bake in the oven for 20-25 minutes or when a toothpick inserted in the centre of the muffins come out clean. Place in wire racks to cool.

6.   Top each muffin with chocolate frosting and sprinkle with mini chocolate chips.

7.   Serve and enjoy!

Easy Vanilla Buttermilk Muffins

This is a classic vanilla muffin recipe that really never goes out of style.

Preparation Time: 15 minutes
Total Time: 40 minutes
Yield: 20servings

Ingredients

2 cups whole wheat flour
1/2cup granulated sugar
2 teaspoons baking powder
1 teaspoon baking soda
1 large egg

1/2 cup sour cream
1/2 cup milk
1/2 cup butter, softened
3 teaspoon vanilla extract

Method

1.   Preheat the oven to 350F. Line muffin trays with baking cups.

2.   In a large bowl, combine whole wheat flour, granulated sugar, baking powder, and baking soda. On a medium speed, add in egg, butter, sour cream, milk, butter, and vanilla until well incorporated but do not over mix.

3.   Pour batter into muffin cups, about 3/4 full.

4.   Bake in the oven for 20 to 25 minutes or when a toothpick inserted in the centre of the muffins comes out clean. Place in wire racks to cool.

5.   Serve and enjoy!

Homemade Orange Muffins with Cinnamon

A delightful muffin recipe with a hint of orange and cinnamon flavor.

Preparation Time: 15 minutes
Total Time: 40 minutes
Yield: 20servings

Ingredients
1/2 cup unsalted butter, softened
1/2cup sugar
1 large egg
1 cup milk
1/4 cup orange juice concentrate

1 teaspoon orange zest (finely grated)
2 cups whole wheat flour
2 teaspoon baking powder
1 teaspoon baking soda
1/2 teaspoon salt

Method

1.   Preheat the oven to 350F.   Line muffin trays with baking cups.

2.   Beat butter and sugar using an electric mixer, scraping the sides as needed.

3.   Add the egg, milk, orange juice concentrate, and orange zest.

4.   Combine the flour, baking powder, and salt in a separate bowl.

5.   Slowly add the flour mixture into the wet ingredients on low speed. Do not over mix.

6.   Pour batter into muffin cups, about 3/4 cup full only.

7.   Bake in the oven for 20-25 minutes or until tested done. Place in wire racks to cool.

8.   Serve or store in airtight container.

Chocolate Chip Muffins

This is an awesome muffin recipe that everybody will surely enjoy.

Preparation Time: 15 minutes
Total Time: 35 minutes
Yield: 20servings

Ingredients
2 cups of all-purpose flour
1/2 cup brown sugar
2 teaspoons baking powder
1 teaspoon baking soda
1/2 teaspoon salt
1/2 cup unsalted butter, melted
1 large egg

1 cup buttermilk
1 teaspoon vanilla extract
1cup semi-sweet chocolate chips
(divided)

Method

1.   Preheat your oven to 350F. Line muffin trays with baking cups.

2.   Combine the all-purpose flour, brown sugar, baking powder, baking soda, and salt in a large bowl.

3.   In a separate bowl, mix together butter, egg, buttermilk, and vanilla extract.

4.   Combine the wet and dry mixture; mix until everything is incorporated and lump-free. Fold in the half of the chocolate chips.

5.   Pour batter into the prepared baking cups, about 3/4 full. Top with remaining chocolate chips.

6.   Bake in the oven for 20-25 minutes or until tested done. Place in wire racks to cool.

7.   Serve and enjoy!

Blueberry Almond Muffins

The sweet-tangy flavor of blueberries is oozing in every bite of this muffin.

Preparation Time: 15minutes
Total Time: 40 minutes
Yield: 20servings

Ingredients
2 cups all-purpose flour
1/3 cup granulated sugar
2teaspoons baking powder
1 teaspoon baking soda
1/2 teaspoon salt
1large egg

1cup buttermilk
1/2cup unsalted butter, melted
1 cup fresh blueberries
1/2 cup slivered almonds

Method

1.   Preheat the oven to 350 F. Line muffin trays with baking cups.

2.   Combine together the flour, granulated sugar, baking powder, baking soda, and salt in a large bowl.

3.   Lightly beat the eggs in a separate bowl. Add the milk and butter.

4.   Mix together the egg mixture and dry ingredients until incorporated and no more lumps.

5.   Fold in blueberries.

6.   Spoon batter evenly onto muffin cups. Sprinkle with slivered almonds.

7.   Bake in the oven for 20-25 minutes or until tested done. Place in wire racks to cool.

8.   Serve and enjoy!

Carrot and Raisin Muffins

*Prepare this ahead of time, these muffins make
a great grab and go breakfast or snack!*

Preparation Time: 15minutes
Total Time: 40 minutes
Yield: 24 servings

Ingredients

2 cups of buckwheat flour
1/2cup of brown sugar
2 teaspoons of baking powder
1 teaspoon of baking soda
1/2teaspoon of salt
1 cup of milk
1/3cup of vegetable oil

1 large egg
1 teaspoon of white vinegar
1 teaspoon of vanilla extract
3/4 cup carrot (grated)
3/4 cup seedless raisins

Method

1.   Preheat the oven to 350F. Line the muffin trays with baking cups.

2.   Combine together the buckwheat flour, brown sugar, baking powder, baking soda, and salt in a large bowl.

3.   In another bowl, mix together the milk, vegetable oil, egg, white vinegar, and vanilla extract using an electric mixer.

4.   Gradually add dry ingredients into the wet mixture and mix until just blended.

5.   Fold in carrots and raisins.

6.   Pour batter into muffin cups, about 3/4 full.

7.   Bake for 20-25 minutes or until tested done. Cool completely on wire racks.

8.   Serve and enjoy!

Les Ilagan

Pumpkin Spice Banana Muffins

A satisfying muffin recipe made with banana, pumpkin puree, and pumpkin spice.

Preparation Time: 15 minutes
Total Time: 40 minutes
Yield: 24 servings

Ingredients

2cups of all-purpose flour
2 teaspoons pumpkin spice
2 teaspoons of baking powder
1 teaspoon of baking soda
1/2 teaspoon salt
2/3 cup of canola oil

1/3 cup of brown sugar
1large egg
1 cup of milk
1/2 cup of pumpkin puree
2 medium ripe bananas (mashed)

Method

1.   Preheat the oven to 350F. Line 2 muffin trays with baking cups.

2.   In a medium mixing bowl, sift together the flour, pumpkin spice, baking powder, baking soda, and salt.

3.   In a separate bowl, combine canola oil, egg, brown sugar, and milk. Mix well.

4.   Stir in pumpkin puree and mashed bananas.

5.   Gradually add the flour mixture and mix until just blended.

6.   Pour batter into the muffin cups, about 3/4 cup full only.

7.   Bake in the oven for 20-25 minutes or until golden brown and tested done. Cool completely on wire racks.

8.   Serve and enjoy!

Buttered Corn Muffins

These wonderful buttered corn muffins are a sure hit! They make a perfect picnic or party item.

Preparation Time: 15 minutes
Total Time: 40 minutes
Yield: 20servings

Ingredients
2 cups all-purpose flour
1/3cupgranulated sugar
2 teaspoons baking powder
1 teaspoon baking soda
1/2 teaspoon salt
3/4 cup unsalted butter, softened

1large egg
1 teaspoon vanilla extract
1/2 cup milk
1/2 cup sour cream
1 cup canned sweet corn kernels

Method

1.   Preheat the oven to 350F.   Line muffin trays with paper cups.

2.   In a large bowl, combine the flour, granulated sugar, baking powder, and baking soda, and salt.

3.   On a medium speed, add in butter, egg, vanilla, milk, and sour cream until smooth. Do not over mix.

4.   Fold in sweet corn kernels.

5.   Spoon batter into the muffin cups, about 3/4 cup full only.

6.   Bake in the oven for 20-25 minutes or until tested done. Place in wire racks to cool.

7.   Serve and Enjoy!

Homemade Almond Muffins

This fantastic almond muffin recipe is truly delicious and satisfying!

Preparation Time: 15minutes
Total Time: 40 minutes
Yield: 18servings

Ingredients

1 cup almond meal
1 cup of whole wheat flour
2 teaspoons of baking powder
1 teaspoon of baking soda
1/2 teaspoon of salt
1/4 cup of almond butter
1/4 cup vegetable oil
1 large egg

1/2 cup of brown sugar
1 teaspoon vanilla extract
1/2 cup water
1/2 cup almond milk
1/2 cup slivered almonds

Method

1.	Preheat the oven to 350 F. Line muffin trays with paper cups.
2.	In a medium bowl, combine almond meal, whole wheat flour, baking powder, baking soda, and salt.
3.	In a separate bowl, mix together the almond butter, oil, egg, sugar, vanilla extract, water, and milk until blended well.
4.	At low speed, gradually add the dry mixture mix until just combined.
5.	Spoon batter into the muffin cups, about 3/4 full. Sprinkle with slivered almonds.
6.	Bake in the oven for 20-25 minutes or when until tested done. Place in wire racks to cool.
7.	Serve and enjoy!

Banana Cashew Muffins

These banana cashew muffins are incredibly delicious!

Preparation Time: 15 minutes
Total Time: 40 minutes
Yield: 22servings

Ingredients

2 cups buckwheat flour
2 teaspoons baking powder
1 teaspoon baking soda
1/2 teaspoon salt
1/3 cup brown sugar
1/3 cup vegetable oil
1 large egg

3 medium ripe bananas (mashed)
1 cup milk
1 teaspoon vanilla extract
1 cup dry roasted cashew nuts

Method

1.   Preheat the oven to 350 F. Line muffin trays with baking cups.
2.   Sift the buckwheat flour, baking powder, baking soda, and salt in a medium bowl.
3.   In a separate bowl, combine together the sugar, oil, egg, and milk.
4.   Slowly add the dry mixture into the wet mixture. Mix until just combined.
5.   Fold in mashed bananas and half of the cashews.
6.   Pour batter into the muffin cups, about 3/4 full. Top with remaining cashews.
7.   Bake in the oven for 20-25 minutes or until tested done. Place in wire racks to cool.
8.   Serve and enjoy.

Yummy Peppermint Chocolate Muffins

Feel the refreshing taste of peppermint in every bite of these chocolate muffins!

Preparation Time: 15 minutes
Total Time: 40 minutes
Yield: 20 servings

Ingredients

1 cup semi-sweet chocolate, melted
1/2cup unsalted butter, melted
1/2 cup brown sugar
1large egg
1 teaspoon pure peppermint extract
2 cups all-purpose flour, sifted

2 teaspoons baking powder
1 teaspoon baking soda
1/2 teaspoon salt
1 cup water

Method

1.   Preheat the oven to 350F.   Line muffin trays with baking cups.

2.   Using an electric mixer, combine melted chocolate, butter, brown sugar, egg, and peppermint extract; beat until well blended.

3.   On low speed, gradually add the flour, baking powder, baking soda, salt, and water. Mix until smooth but do not overdo.

4.   Spoon batter into muffin cups, about 3/4 cup full.

5.   Bake in the oven for 20 to 25 minutes or until tested done. Place in wire racks to cool.

6.   Serve and enjoy!

Cherry Almond Meal Muffin

Soft and fluffy muffins with almond meal and cherries.

Preparation Time: 15minutes
Total Time: 40 minutes
Yield: 20servings

Ingredients

1 cup almond meal
1 cup all-purpose flour
2teaspoons baking powder
1 teaspoon baking soda
1/2 teaspoon salt
1/2 cup melted butter (unsalted)
1/2 cup granulated sugar
1 large egg

1 cup milk
1 teaspoon vanilla extract
1 cup fresh cherries (pitted)

Method

1.   Preheat the oven to 350F. Line muffin trays with baking cups.

2.   Combine almond meal, flour, baking powder, baking soda, and salt in a medium mixing bowl. Set aside.

3.   In a separate bowl, cream butter and sugar until lightly fluffy using an electric mixer at a medium high speed. Add the egg, milk, and vanilla extract.

4.   Fold in cherries.

5.   Spoon batter into muffin cups, about 3/4 full only.

6.   Bake in the oven for 20 to 25 minutes or until tested done. Place in a wire rack to cool.

7.   Serve and enjoy!

Fluffy Chocolate Muffins

This chocolate muffin recipe is so fluffy and yummy!

Preparation Time: 15minutes
Total Time: 40 minutes
Yield: 24servings

Ingredients
2 cups of all-purpose flour
2teaspoons baking powder
1 teaspoon baking soda
1/2 teaspoon salt
1/2 cup unsalted butter, softened
1/2cupgranulated sugar
6 ounces dark chocolate, melted

1 teaspoon pure vanilla extract
1 large egg
1/2 cup yogurt
1/2 cup milk
Chocolate frosting (to serve)
Candy sprinkles (to serve)

Method

1.   Preheat in the oven to 350F. Line muffin trays with baking cups.

2.   Mix together the all-purpose flour, baking powder, baking soda and salt in a medium bowl.

3.   In a separate bowl, cream together butter and sugar until light and fluffy using an electric mixer. On a medium speed, add in melted chocolate and vanilla extract; beat until well blended.

4.   Add the egg, yogurt, and milk. Mix well.

5.   Add the flour mixture gradually and continue mixing until just incorporated.

6.   Spoon batter into muffin cups, about 3/4 cup full only.

7.   Bake in the oven for 20-25 minutes or until tested done. Place in wire racks to cool.

8.   Top with chocolate frosting and candy sprinkles.

9.   Serve and enjoy!

Choco Walnut Muffins

A delightful chocolate muffin recipe with walnuts.

Preparation Time: 15minutes
Total Time: 40 minutes
Yield: 20servings

Ingredients
1/2cup butter, at room temperature
1/2cup granulated sugar
1 large egg
1 teaspoon pure vanilla extract
1 3/4 cups whole wheat flour

2/3 cup pure cocoa powder
2 teaspoons baking powder
1 teaspoon baking soda
1 cup water
3/4 cup walnuts (coarsely chopped)

Method

1.   Preheat the oven to 350F. Line muffin trays with baking cups.

2.   In the bowl of an electric mixer, cream the butter and sugar using paddle attachment on medium-high speed. Add the egg and vanilla.

3.   Combine whole wheat flour, cocoa powder, baking powder, and baking soda in a separate bowl.

4.   Add dry the flour mixture gradually alternating with water on low speed until just combined. Fold in chopped walnuts.

5.   Spoon batter into muffin cups, about 3/4 cup full only.

6.   Bake for 20-25 minutes or until tested done. Place in wire racks to cool.

7.   Serve and enjoy!

Blueberry and Vanilla Muffin

This easy and tasty muffin recipe with blueberries and vanilla will surely brighten up your day.

Preparation Time: 15 minutes
Total Time: 40 minutes
Yield: 20 servings

Ingredients
2 cups all-purpose flour
2 teaspoons baking powder
1 teaspoon baking soda
1/4 teaspoon salt
1large egg
1/3 cup vegetable oil
1 cup water

1 teaspoon white vinegar
1 teaspoon vanilla extract
1 cup blueberries

Method

1.   Preheat the oven to 350 F. Line muffin trays with baking cups.

2.   In a large bowl, combine the egg, oil, sugar, water, vinegar, and vanilla extract. Mix well.

3.   Sift the flour, baking powder, baking soda, and salt; add into the wet mixture. Mix until just combined. Fold in blueberries.

4.   Spoon batter into the muffin cups, about 3/4 full.

5.   Bake in the oven for 20-25 minutes or until tested done. Place in wire racks to cool.

6.   Serve and enjoy.

Banana Oat and Raisin Muffins

This muffin recipe made with banana, oat bran, and raisins is packed with fiber and awesome flavors.

Preparation Time: 15minutes
Total Time: 45 minutes
Yield: 24 servings

Ingredients
1 1/4 cups whole-wheat flour
3/4 cup oat bran
2 teaspoons baking powder
1 teaspoon baking soda

1 teaspoon ground cinnamon
1/2 teaspoon salt
1/3 cup vegetable oil
1/3 cups brown sugar
2 large eggs
3/4 cup buttermilk
1 teaspoon vanilla extract
3 medium ripe bananas (mashed)
2/3 cup seedless raisins

Method

1.   Preheat the oven to 350 F. Line muffin trays with paper cups.

2.   Sift the whole wheat flour, oat bran, baking powder, baking soda, cinnamon, and salt. Set aside.

3.   In a large bowl, mix together the vegetable oil, brown sugar, eggs, buttermilk, and vanilla extract using an electric mixer on medium speed until blended well.

4.   Slowly add in the flour mixture, mixing just until combined.

5.   Fold in mashed bananas and raisins. Fill each muffin cup, about 3/4 full.

6.   Bake in the oven for 20 to 25 minutes, or until tested done. Cool in wire racks.

7.   Serve and enjoy.

Coconut and Lemon Muffins

If you love the taste of coconuts, try this wonderful muffin recipe! It is great with coffee or tea.

Preparation Time: 15minutes
Total Time: 40 minutes
Yield: 18 pieces

Ingredients
1 large egg, lightly beaten
1/4 cup coconut oil
1/4 cup granulated sugar
1 cup milk
2 tablespoons lemon juice
1 1/4 cups whole wheat flour

3/4 cup coconut flour
2 teaspoons baking powder
1 teaspoon baking soda
1/4 teaspoon salt
1/2 cup coconut flakes (for topping)

Method

1.   Preheat your oven to 350 F. Line muffin trays with paper cups.

2.   In a large bowl, whisk together the egg, coconut oil, granulated sugar, and milk and lemon juice until smooth using an electric mixer.

3.   Add the whole wheat flour, coconut flour, baking powder, baking soda, and salt. Mix until just combined.

4.   Spoon batter into the muffin cups, about 3/4 full. Sprinkle with coconut flakes.

5.   Bake in the oven for 20-25 minutes until tested done. Place in wire racks to cool.

6.   Serve or store in airtight container.

Poppy Seed Muffins with Applesauce

A low-fat muffin recipe that is high in fiber and taste great too!

Preparation Time: 15minutes
Total Time: 40 minutes
Yield: 18 pieces

Ingredients

2 cups whole wheat flour
2teaspoons baking powder
1teaspoon baking soda
1 teaspoon cinnamon
2 large eggs

3/4 cup buttermilk
1/2 cup applesauce
1/2 cup sugar
1/4 cup poppy seeds

Method

1.   Preheat the oven to 350F. Line the muffin trays with baking cups.

2.   Sift the whole wheat flour, baking powder, baking soda, and cinnamon in a medium bowl. Set aside.

3.   Using an electric mixer, combine together the eggs, buttermilk, applesauce, and sugar until smooth.

4.   Gradually add in flour mixture and mix until just combined. Fold in poppy seeds.

5.   Spoon batter into baking cups, about 3/4full.

6.   Bake in the oven for 20 to 25 minutes or until tested done. Place in wire racks to cool.

7.   Serve and enjoy.

Pumpkin and Pecan Muffins

This pumpkin muffin recipe with pecans makes a perfect thanksgiving treat!

Preparation Time: 15minutes
Total Time: 40 minutes
Yield: 24servings

Ingredients

2 cups whole wheat flour
1 teaspoon baking powder
1 teaspoon baking soda
1/2 teaspoon cinnamon, ground
1/4 teaspoon ginger, ground

1/4 teaspoon nutmeg, ground
1/4 teaspoon cloves, ground
1/4 teaspoon salt
1 large egg
1/3 cup vegetable oil, unsalted
1/2cup brown sugar
3/4 cup milk
1/2 pumpkin puree
3/4 cup pecans (coarsely chopped)
Diced cooked pumpkin (to serve –
optional)

Method

1.   Preheat your oven to 350F. Line the muffin trays with paper cups.

2.   Sift the whole wheat flour, baking powder, baking soda, cinnamon, ginger, nutmeg, cloves, and salt in a medium bowl. Mix well.

3.   In a separate bowl, mix together the egg, oil, brown sugar, and milk.

4.   Gradually add the dry mixture, mix until just combined. Fold in pumpkin puree and pecans.

5.   Spoon batter into baking cups, about 3/4full.

6.   Bake in the oven for 20-25 minutes until tested done. Place in wire racks to cool.

7.   Serve or store in airtight container.

Banana Walnut Muffins

A great tasting and moist banana muffin recipe with walnuts.

Preparation Time: 15minutes
Total Time: 45 minutes
Yield: 20 servings

Ingredients
2 cups all-purpose flour
2 teaspoons baking powder
1 teaspoon baking soda
1/2 teaspoon cinnamon
1/2 teaspoon nutmeg
1/2 teaspoon salt

1/2cup applesauce
1/3 cup brown sugar
1 teaspoon vanilla extract
1 large egg
1cup milk
3 medium ripe bananas (mashed)
1 cup walnuts (chopped)

Method

1.   Preheat the oven to 350F. Line the muffin trays with paper cups.
2.   Sift together the flour, baking powder, baking soda, cinnamon, nutmeg, and salt in a medium bowl.
3.   Combine the applesauce, brown sugar, vanilla extract, egg, and milk in a large bowl.
4.   Gradually add the flour mixture into the wet mixture. Mixing just until combined.
5.   Fold in the mashed banana and half of the walnuts.
6.   Spoon batter into baking cups, about   3/4full.Top   with   remaining walnuts.
7.   Bake in the oven for 20-25 minutes or until tested done. Place in wire racks to cool.

8.   Serve and enjoy.

Delicious Ban apple Muffins with Almonds

This awesome muffin recipe with banana and apple is simply irresistible!

Preparation Time: 15minutes
Total Time: 40 minutes
Yield: 24 servings

Ingredients

1/2 cup applesauce
1/4cup brown sugar
2 large eggs
6 oz.plain yogurt

21/4 cups whole wheat flour
2 teaspoons baking powder
1 teaspoon baking soda
1 teaspoon apple pie spice
1/2 teaspoon salt
2 medium ripe bananas (mashed)
1 cup dry roasted almonds (coarsely chopped)

Method

1.   Preheat the oven to 350F. Line the muffin trays with paper cups.

2.   In a large bowl, mix together applesauce, brown sugar, eggs, and yogurt using an electric mixer set to a medium speed for 2 minutes. Set aside.

3.   Sift the whole wheat flour, baking powder, baking soda, apple pie spice, and salt in a separate bowl.

4.   On low speed, gradually add the flour and spice mixture and mix until just combined.

5.   Fold in mashed banana and almonds.

6.   Spoon batter into baking cups, about 3/4full.

7.   Bake in the oven for 20-25 minutes or until tested done. Place in wire racks to cool.

8.   Serve and enjoy.

3

Homemade Blackberry and Oat Muffins

This muffin recipe is packed with fiber and the fresh flavor of blackberries in each and every bite!

Preparation Time: 15 minutes
Total Time: 40 minutes
Yield: 24servings

Ingredients
1/2cup vegetable oil
1/2 cup brown sugar
1 teaspoon pure vanilla extract
2 large eggs

1 1/2cups all-purpose flour
2/3 cup rolled oats
2teaspoons baking powder
1 teaspoon baking soda
1/2 teaspoon salt
1cup buttermilk
1 1/2cupsblackberries

Method

1.   Preheat the oven to 350F.   Line muffin trays with paper cups.

2.   In a large bowl, combine the vegetable oil, sugar, vanilla extract, and eggs. Mix well.

3.   Combine all dry ingredients in a separate bowl. Gradually add the dry mixture into the wet mixture. Do not over mix.

4.   Fold in blackberries.

5.   Spoon batter into baking cups, about 3/4full.

6.   Bake in the oven for 20-25 minutes or until tested done. Place in wire racks to cool.

7.   Serve and enjoy.

Vanilla Almond Muffin

A wonderful muffin recipe made with almonds and a hint of vanilla.

Preparation Time: 15minutes
Total Time: 40 minutes
Yield: 18servings

Ingredients

1 cup almond milk
1/2 cup unsalted butter (softened)
1/2 cup granulated sugar
1 teaspoon vanilla extract
1 large egg
1 cup all-purpose flour, sifted

1 cup almond flour, sifted
2 teaspoons baking powder
1teaspoon baking soda
1/2teaspoon salt
1/2 cup slivered almonds

Method

1.   Preheat the oven to 350F. Line the muffin trays with paper cups.

2.   In a large mixing bowl, mix together butter, sugar, vanilla, egg, and almond milk using an electric mixer set to medium speed.

3.   Combine all-purpose flour, almond flour, baking powder, baking soda, and salt in a separate bowl. Slowly add dry mixture onto the wet mixture and continue mixing until smooth. Do not over mix.

4.   Spoon batter into baking cups, about 3/4 full. Top with slivered almonds.

5.   Bake for 20 to 25 minutes or until tested done. Place in wire racks to cool.

6.   Serve and enjoy.

Les Ilagan

Easy Banana Oat Muffin

If you are looking for a treat that is also healthy, this is the recipe for you! It is packed with fiber from the whole wheat flour, banana, and oats.

Preparation Time: 15minutes
Total Time: 45minutes
Yield: 24servings

Ingredients
1 1/2 cup whole wheat flour
1/2 cup oat bran
2teaspoons baking powder
1 teaspoon baking soda

1/2 teaspoon salt
1/2 teaspoon all-spice
1/2cup apple sauce
1/2cup brown sugar
2 medium eggs
1 cup buttermilk
2 medium bananas (mashed)

Method

1.   Preheat the oven to 350 F. Line the muffin trays with baking cups.

2.   Combine flour, oat bran, baking powder, baking soda, salt, and all-spice in a medium bowl.

3.   Whisk together applesauce, brown sugar, eggs, and milk in a separate bowl.

4.   Add the flour mixture gradually and mix until just blended.

5.   Spoon batter into baking cups, about 3/4 full.

6.   Bake in the oven for 20-25 minutes or until tested done. Place in wire racks to cool.

7.   Serve and enjoy.

Coffee Choco Muffins

A perfect treat for all coffee and chocolate lovers!

Preparation Time: 15minutes
Total Time: 40
Yield: 20servings

Ingredients

2 cups of all-purpose flour
2 teaspoons of baking powder
1 teaspoon of baking soda
1 1/2 teaspoon instant coffee granules
1/2 teaspoon of salt
1/2 cup of unsalted butter, softened

1/2 cup of brown sugar
1 large egg
1 cup milk
1 cup mini chocolate chips

Method

1.　　Preheat the oven to 350 F. Line the muffin trays with paper cups.

2.　　Mix together the flour, baking powder, baking soda, coffee, and salt in a medium bowl.

3.　　Using an electric mixer on medium speed, combine butter, brown sugar, egg, and milk in a large bowl.

4.　　Gradually add the flour mixture and mix until just combined. Fold in half of the chocolate chips.

5.　　Spoon batter into muffin cups, about 3/4 full. Top with remaining chocolate chips.

6.　　Bake in the oven for 20-25 minutes or until tested done. Place in wire racks to cool.

7.　　Serve or store in airtight container.

Luscious Cranberry Muffin with Flaxseed

A lovely muffin recipe with cranberries and flaxseeds.

Preparation Time: 15minutes
Total Time: 40 minutes
Yield: 24servings

Ingredients

2 cups of whole wheat flour
2 teaspoons of baking powder
1 teaspoon of baking soda
1/2 teaspoon of salt
1/2 cup of butter
1/2 cup of granulated sugar
2 medium eggs

6 oz.vanilla yogurt
1 cup fresh cranberries
1/4 cup flaxseeds

Method

1.   Preheat your oven to 350 F. Line the muffin trays with paper cups.

2.   Combine the flour, baking powder, baking soda, and salt in a medium bowl.

3.   Using an electric mixer on medium-high speed, cream butter and sugar in a large bowl until smooth.

4.   Add the eggs one at a time and then the yogurt. Mix well.

5.   Gradually add the flour mixture and mix until just combined. Fold in the cranberries and flaxseeds.

6.   Spoon batter into muffin cups, about 3/4 full.

7.   Bake in the oven for 20-25 minutes or until tested done. Place in wire racks to cool.

8.   Serve or store in airtight container.

Easy Nutella Muffins

Moist and soft muffins with topped with Nutella and hazelnuts.

Preparation Time: 15 minutes
Total Time: 40 minutes
Yield: 20servings

Ingredients

2 cups all-purpose flour (sifted)
1/2 teaspoon salt
2 teaspoons baking powder
1 teaspoon baking soda
1/2cup butter
1/2cup white sugar
1 teaspoon vanilla extract

2medium eggs
1 cup buttermilk
Nutella, for topping
Chopped hazelnuts, for topping

Method

1.   Preheat your oven to 350F. Line the muffin trays with paper cups.

2.   In a large bowl, with an electric mixer set to medium speed, beat together the butter, white sugar, and vanilla extract until smooth and fluffy.

3.   Add the eggs one at a time until well combined.

4.   Combine all dry ingredients in a separate bowl.

5.   Slowly add in the dry mixture into the wet mixture and beat on low speed until just combined.

6.   Spoon batter into baking cups, about 3/4full.

7.   Bake in the oven for 20 minutes or until tested done. Place in wire racks to cool.

8.   Spread 1 tablespoon of Nutella evenly onto each muffin and sprinkle with chopped hazelnuts.

9.   Serve immediately and enjoy.

Orange Blueberry Muffins with Hemp Seeds

A yummy muffin recipe that combines the flavor of orange and blueberry.

Preparation Time: 15minutes
Total Time: 45 minutes
Yield: 18servings

Ingredients

2cups all-purpose flour
2teaspoons baking powder
1 teaspoon baking soda
1/2 teaspoon salt
3/4 cup milk
1/2 cup vegetable oil

1/3cup honey
1/4orange juice concentrates
1 large egg
1 cup fresh blueberries
1/4 cup hemp seeds

Method

1.   Preheat your oven to 350F. Line the muffin trays with paper cups.

2.   In a large mixing bowl, combine the all-purpose flour, baking powder, baking soda, and salt.

3.   Combine all the liquid ingredients in a separate bowl.

4.   Gradually add the flour mixture and mix until just blended.

5.   Fold in blueberries and hemp seeds.

6.   Spoon batter into muffin cups, about 3/4 full.

7.   Bake in the oven for 20-25 minutes or until muffins are tested done. Cool in wire racks.

8.   Serve and enjoy.

Homemade Muffins with Sour Cream

Fluffy and tasty muffins in minutes!

Preparation Time: 15minutes
Total Time: 40 minutes
Yield: 20servings

Ingredients
1/2 cup unsalted butter
1/2 cup white sugar
2 medium eggs
1/2cup milk
1/2 sour cream
1 teaspoon pure vanilla extract

2 cups all-purpose flour (sifted)
2 teaspoon baking powder
1 teaspoon baking soda
1/2 teaspoon salt

Method

1.   Preheat the oven to 350 F. Line the muffin tin with paper cups.

2.   In a medium bowl, with an electric mixer set to medium speed, cream butter and sugar.

3.   Add the eggs one at a time. Then add the milk, sour cream, and vanilla.

4.   Combine all-purpose flour, baking powder, baking soda, and salt in a separate bowl then slowly add into the wet mixture and mix until smooth. Do not over mix.

5.   Pour batter into baking cups, about 3/4 full.

6.   Bake in the oven for 20 to 25 minutes or until tested done. Place in wire racks to cool.

7.   Serve and enjoy.

Banana Peanut Butter Muffins

This stress-free homemade muffin recipe with banana and peanut butter is great for breakfast or snack.

Preparation Time: 15minutes
Total Time: 40 minutes
Yield: 20servings

Ingredients

1/4 cup softened butter
1/4 cup brown sugar
1/2 cup peanut butter
2 medium eggs
2cups sifted all-purpose flour

2 teaspoons baking powder
1 teaspoon baking soda
1 cup milk
2 medium ripe bananas (mashed)
1/2 cup dry roasted peanuts (chopped)

Method

1.   Preheat the oven to 350 F. Line the muffin trays with paper cups.

2.   In a large bowl, with an electric mixer set to medium speed, cream together the softened butter, brown sugar, and peanut butter until well blended.

3.   Add eggs one at a time.

4.   Gradually add the dry ingredients alternately with milk; mix until just combined.

5.   Fold in mashed bananas.

6.   Pour batter into baking cups, about 3/4 full. Top with chopped peanuts.

7.   Bake in the oven for 20-25 minutes or until tested done. Place in wire racks to cool.

8.   Serve and enjoy.

Sweet Chocolate Muffins with Honey

These sweet muffins will surely satisfy those sweet cravings.

Preparation Time: 15 minutes
Total Time: 40 minutes
Yield: 20 servings

Ingredients

1/3 cup vegetable oil
1/3 cup honey
1/2 cup semi-sweet chocolate melted
1 large egg
1 1/2cups all-purpose flour

1/2 cup buckwheat flour
2 teaspoons baking powder
1 teaspoon baking soda
1 teaspoon salt
1 cup hot water

Method

1.   Preheat the oven to 350 F. Line the muffin tin with paper cups.

2.   In a large bowl, beat the egg then add the oil, honey, and melted chocolate.

3.   Gradually add the dry ingredients alternately with hot water; mix until combined well.

4.   Spoon batter into muffin cups, about 3/4 full.

5.   Bake in the oven for 20-25 minutes or until tested done. Place in wire racks to cool.

6.   Serve and enjoy.

Buttermilk Muffins with Chocolate Chips

These light and fluffy muffins with chocolate chips are perfect with coffee or tea.

Preparation Time: 15 minutes
Total Time: 35 minutes
Yield: 20 servings

Ingredients

1/3 cup vegetable oil
1/2cup agave nectar
1 teaspoon pure vanilla extract
2 large eggs
2 cups sifted all-purpose flour

2 teaspoons baking powder
1 teaspoon baking soda
1 cup buttermilk
2/3 cup mini chocolate chips

Method

1.   Preheat the oven to 375 F.   Line the muffin trays with paper cups.

2.   In a large bowl, with an electric mixer set to medium speed, combine together the vegetable oil, agave nectar, and vanilla until blended well. Add eggs one at a time.

3.   Gradually add the flour, baking powder, and baking soda alternately with buttermilk; mix until just combined.

4.   Fold in mini chocolate chips.

5.   Spoon batter into baking cups, about 3/4 full.

6.   Bake in the oven for about 20 minutes or until tested done. Place in wire racks to cool.

7.   Serve and enjoy.

Deep Dark Chocolate Muffins

This muffin recipe has a rich chocolatey flavor.

Preparation Time: 15 minutes
Total Time: 35 minutes
Yield: 24 servings

Ingredients

2 large eggs
1/2 cup dark chocolate (melted)
3/4 cup brown sugar
1/2 cup vegetable oil
2 cups all-purpose flour
1/2cup cocoa powder
1 teaspoon baking powder

1 teaspoon baking soda
1/2 teaspoon salt
1 cup hot water
1 teaspoon white vinegar

Method

1.	Preheat the oven to 350 F. Line the muffin trays with baking cups.

2.	In a large bowl, beat the eggs using an electric mixer. Add the melted chocolate, brown sugar, and vegetable oil. Mix well.

3.	Sift together the dry ingredients and gradually add into the wet mixture alternately with hot water. Mix until just blended. Stir in white vinegar.

4.	Spoon batter into muffin cups, about 3/4 full.

5.	Bake in the oven for about 20-25 minutes or until tested done. Place in wire racks to cool.

6.	Serve or store in airtight container.

Cheesy Muffins

This cheese muffin recipe is so delicious and filling.

Preparation Time: 15 minutes
Total Time: 35 minutes
Yield: 24 servings

Ingredients

1/2 cup sugar
1/3 cup vegetable oil
1 cup milk
2 large eggs
2 1/4 cups whole wheat flour
2 teaspoons baking powder
1 teaspoon baking soda

1/4 cup parmesan cheese
1/2 cup cheddar cheese

Method

1.   Preheat the oven to 375 F. Line muffin trays with paper cups.

2.   Beat the eggs in a large mixing bowl. Add the sugar and oil. Mix well.

3.   Sift together all dry ingredients and gradually add into the wet mixture alternately with milk. Mix until just blended.

4.   Fold in parmesan cheese and cheddar cheese.

5.   Spoon batter into muffin cups, about 3/4 full.

6.   Bake in the oven for about 20 minutes or until tested done. Place in wire racks to cool.

7.   Serve or store in airtight container.

Choco Coffee Muffins with Cinnamon

This delightful chocolate muffin recipe is really flavorful.

Preparation Time: 15 minutes
Total Time: 35 minutes
Yield: 24 servings

Ingredients

2 large eggs
1/2 cup semi-sweet chocolate (melted)
1/3 cup granulated sugar
1/3 cup vegetable oil
2 1/4 cups all-purpose flour
1/3 cup cocoa powder

2 teaspoons baking powder
1 teaspoon baking soda
2 teaspoons instant coffee granules
1 teaspoon cinnamon, ground
1/2 teaspoon salt
1/2 cup buttermilk
1/2 cup hot water

Method

1.	Preheat the oven to 375 F. Line the muffin trays with paper cups.

2.	In a large bowl, beat the eggs using an electric mixer. Add the melted chocolate, sugar, and vegetable oil. Mix well.

3.	Sift together the dry ingredients and gradually add into the wet mixture alternately with buttermilk and water. Mix until just combined.

4.	Spoon batter into muffin cups, about 3/4 full.

5.	Bake in the oven for about 20 minutes or until tested done. Place in wire racks to cool.

6.	Serve or store in airtight container.

Super Moist Banana and Pumpkin Muffins

This muffin recipe makes a perfect lunchbox or picnic item.

Preparation Time: 15 minutes
Total Time: 35 minutes
Yield: 24 servings

Ingredients

1/2cup applesauce
1/3 cup muscovado or brown sugar
2 large eggs
3/4 cup buttermilk
2 medium ripe bananas (mashed)
1/2 cup pumpkin puree

2cups all-purpose flour
2 teaspoons baking powder
1 teaspoon baking soda
1 teaspoon pumpkin spice
1/2 teaspoon salt

Method

1.   Preheat the oven to 375F. Line the muffin trays with paper cups.

2.   Using a wire whisk, mix together applesauce, muscovado, and eggs in a large bowl.

3.   Add buttermilk, mashed bananas, and pumpkin puree.

4.   Stir in the dry ingredients just until blended.

5.   Spoon batter into muffin cups evenly, about 3/4 full.

6.   Bake in the oven for about 20 minutes or until tested done. Place in wire racks to cool.

7.   Serve or store in airtight container.

Cheese Muffins with Vanilla

A cheesy muffin recipe with a hint of vanilla.

Preparation Time: 15 minutes
Total Time: 35 minutes
Yield: 20 servings

Ingredients

2 cups all-purpose flour
2 teaspoon baking powder
1 teaspoon baking soda
1/4 teaspoon salt
1/2 cup unsalted butter
2 large eggs
1/2 cup condensed milk
1/2 cup buttermilk

1 teaspoon pure vanilla extract
1cup Velveeta cheese (grated)

Method

1.   Preheat the oven to 375 F. Line the muffin trays with paper cups.

2.   Combine the flour, baking powder, baking soda, and salt in a large bowl.

3.   In a separate bowl, beat the eggs. Add the condensed milk, buttermilk, butter, and vanilla extract.

4.   Gradually add the flour mixture and mix until just combined.

5.   Fold in Velveeta cheese.

6.   Spoon batter into muffin cups, about 3/4 full.

7.   Bake in the oven for about 20 minutes or until tested done. Cool in wire racks.

8.   Serve and enjoy.

Cranberry Pineapple Muffins with Walnuts

This muffin recipe with cranberries, pineapple, and walnuts is a sure hit with the kids!

Preparation Time: 15 minutes
Total Time: 35 minutes
Yield: 24 servings

Ingredients

2 cups all-purpose flour
2 teaspoons baking powder
1 teaspoon baking soda
1/2 teaspoon salt
1/2 cup granulated sugar
1/2 cup sour cream
1/2 cup milk

1/2 cup vegetable oil
1 large egg
1 cup cranberries
1/2 cup crushed pineapple
3/4 cup walnuts (coarsely chopped)

Method

1.   Preheat in the oven to 375 F. Line the muffin trays with baking cups.

2.   In a large mixing bowl, combine the flour, baking powder, baking soda, salt, and granulated sugar.

3.   Mix together all the wet ingredients in a separate bowl.

4.   Combine the dry and wet ingredients until just blended.

5.   Fold in cranberries, crushed pineapple, and walnuts.

6.   Spoon batter into muffin cups, about 3/4 full.

7.   Bake in the oven for about 20 minutes or until tested done. Cool in wire racks.

8.   Serve or store in airtight container.

Homemade Bran Muffins with Flaxseeds

A simple and easy muffin recipe that is also healthy!

Preparation Time: 15 minutes
Total Time: 35 minutes
Yield: 20 servings

Ingredients
1 cup of whole wheat flour
1 cup oat bran
1/2 cup of brown sugar
2teaspoons of baking powder
1 teaspoon of baking soda

1/2 teaspoon of salt
2 large eggs
1 cup buttermilk
2/3 cup of applesauce
1 teaspoon of pure vanilla extract
1/4 cup flaxseeds

Method

1.   Preheat the oven to 375 F. Line the muffin trays with paper cups.

2.   Combine together the flour, oat bran, brown sugar, baking powder, baking soda, and salt in a large bowl.

3.   In another bowl, mix together the eggs, buttermilk, applesauce, and vanilla extract using an electric mixer set to medium speed.

4.   Gradually add the dry ingredients and flaxseeds. Mix until well blended. Do not over mix.

5.   Spoon batter into muffin cups, about 3/4 full.

6.   Bake for about 20 minutes or until tested done. Place in wire racks to cool.

7.   Serve and enjoy.

Orange Ginger Muffins

This is a delightful muffin recipe made with orange and ginger.

Preparation Time: 15 minutes
Total Time: 35 minutes
Yield: 24 servings

Ingredients

2¼ cups whole wheat flour
2 teaspoons baking powder
1 teaspoon baking soda
1/2 teaspoon salt
2 teaspoons ginger powder
2 large eggs
1/2 cup granulated sugar
1/2 cup vegetable oil

1/2 cup orange juice concentrate
6 oz. plain yogurt
1 tablespoon orange zest

Method

1.   Preheat the oven to 350 F. Line the muffin trays with paper cups.

2.   Combine whole wheat flour, baking powder, baking soda, salt, and ginger powder in a medium bowl. Set aside.

3.   In a large bowl, beat the eggs set to medium speed for 1 minute using an electric mixer. Add the sugar gradually, then the oil orange juice concentrate, yogurt, and zest. Mix well.

4.   At low speed, add the flour mixture until just combined.

5.   Spoon batter to muffin cups, about 3/4 full.

6.   Bake in the oven for 20-25 minutes or until tested done. Place in wire racks to cool.

7.   Serve and enjoy.

Yummy Party Chocolate Muffins

This chocolate muffin recipe with candy sprinkles is perfect for kiddie parties.

Preparation Time: 15 minutes
Total Time: 35 minutes
Yield: 20 servings

Ingredients

2 cups whole wheat flour
1/2 cup brown sugar
2 teaspoons baking powder
1teaspoon baking soda
1/2 cup cocoa powder
1/2 teaspoon salt

1 large egg
1/2 cup bitter sweet chocolate (melted)
1 cup hot water
1/2 cup vegetable oil

Method

1.   Preheat the oven to 375F. Line the muffin trays with baking cups.

2.   In a large bowl, combine flour, sugar, baking powder, baking soda, cocoa powder, and salt.

3.   Combine all wet ingredients in a separate bowl. Mix well.

4.   Gradually add the flour mixture and stir until combined. Do not over mix.

5.   Spoon batter into muffin cups, about 3/4 full. Top with candy sprinkles.

6.   Bake in the oven for about 20 minutes or until tested done. Place in wire racks to cool.

7.   Serve and enjoy!

Printed in Great Britain
by Amazon